NINE LIVES MATTER

DIMITRI KATAKALOS

NINE LIVES MATTER

Dimitri Katakalos
Nine Lives Matter

All rights reserved
Copyright © 2025 by Dimitri Katakalos

This is a work of fiction. Names, characters, places and incidents either are products of the author's imagination or are used fictitiously. Any resemblance to actual events or locales or persons, living or dead, is entirely coincidental.

Published by Spines

ISBN: 979-8-89691-465-5

"Take your time and think things over. You have done good work here, and I know you don't deserve what has happened to you." He knew what Dr. Milstein was telling him meant his exit from the internship he had been working to complete for the last year and a half. Now, here at the end, Apostolos knew there was no way he could defend himself from the accusation of inappropriate speech he stood accused of from a sixteen-year-old female patient. The administration of Encino Groves never tolerated any accusations of its employees: fire them and forget it. *Two Master's degrees, three internships, four rehabs mental health worker grunt working, and a year of co-facilitating adolescent sex offender groups, a Clinical Liasion for Life Values' homeless people with psychotic conditions in Phoenix, and now I am the "perpetrator?"*

"Dr. Milstein," Ioan started his answer.

"Just 'Jake,' Ioan. Please, I am still your friend. I know you did nothing wrong," Milstein replied. His face expressed serious concern and equal disappointment for Apostolos. Ioan recalled his first visit to Milstein's office two years earlier when the office had the scent of the pipe tobacco the elder kept in a glass humidor on his desk. *Was the scent still present(?)*, he wondered, or was he imagining a simulacrum of it.

"The administration insists we do thorough psychosocial intakes and I have never strayed from asking direct questions in my interviews. Now 'Me Too' puts a target on my back any time I ask about the private behavior that a sexually active adolescent patient has engaged in," Apostolos dryly confessed.

"You have had a life full of experiences before you came to us. You are a keen observer of human behavior. There are other jobs for you to do beyond this clinic," Milstein voiced with hope and encouragement. "Just as there are people living dysfunctional lives, there are institutions with dysfunctional administrations."

Apostolos stood up and extended his hand to Milstein.

"Thank you, Jake. I will never forget what a generous mentor and best friend you have been."

"It's not over yet – our friendship. Please stay in touch," as Milstein solemnly pressed the flesh and bone. Ioan wanted to hug this surrogate grandfather for all his years of guidance and moral support, but that had never been their style. Ioan looked gratefully into the old man's eyes, turned and left the room, reaching for the door.

"Leave it open. My door will always be open for you, Ioan," Milstein called out as Apostolos proceeded down the hallway to the exit.

Many miles away in Ozuna, Texas, Rachel gathered her children together: "Come on, kids, it's time to watch the movie."

It had been a long day already. Rachel and her husband, Gustavo, had been up before dawn. The motel they ran had limited rooms available. Most of them needed remodeling. Gustavo had worked on remodeling most of the available spaces: lighting, plumbing, and new/old furnishings from his brother-in-law's used furniture warehouse. For him it was another day of working to make things work and running to the hardware store when new problems with fittings or materials presented mistakes in his work from the day before. Rachel had been pushing her two teenage daughters into getting the laundry done, and then to work on their home-school assignments while the washing machines cycled.

Deborah was feeling hot even as it was sixty cool degrees. Only the ambient heat of the television and other large home appliances moderated the indoor temperature. She had rejoined her mother's new family two years ago at age twelve. At three years old, her father, Lionel, had picked her up for a weekend visit as the final child custody disposition was still being processed. For the next eleven years, she lived with him in Cleveland, Texas, on the northern edge of Houston, and he ignored the county court's summons. He never responded to Rachel's pleas to have Deborah returned during her early to middle childhood years. The Crockett County court had ruled in Rachel's favor, but no other actions were ever taken by the court. Her childhood became a series of childcare centers, revolving babysitters, and hours of latch-key after-school life. Lionel worked long hours as a project manager for new apartment contractors. Deborah was up nearly every day. She had often fell asleep alone on their living room couch as television light blared on.

Now, after years of special education modules and some after-school prosocial group therapy sessions, Deborah was angry and frustrated. She was especially angry at her mother who had forbade her to see Jonah, a young roughneck who worked near Midland. He had been renting a room at the motel. Together, they had just begun a sexual relationship, which Deborah had denied to her stepfather when he confronted her. Her younger sister, Esther, had told Gustavo in passing that Deborah had been skipping out of home studies to spend time with Jonah.

Today, the family was celebrating Miriam's seventh birthday. The family was gathering to watch Miriam's and Esther's favorite Miyazaki movie, *Spirited* Away. It was up to Deborah to load the DVD.

"I can't find it," she announced.

"I left out on the coffee table," Rachel called out from the kitchen. Together, Deborah's three younger sisters called out that "it's not here/there," their voices harmonizing together.

Gustavo came out of the sister's bedroom brandishing the DVD: "It was in your backpack. How did it get there, Deborah?"

"I'm going to kill you!" Deborah yelled, rushing towards Gustavo with tightly clenched fists raised for the attack.

Rachel came up behind Deborah, reaching for her

forearm to stop her. Deborah swung around and punched Rachel, yelling, "Let me kill the bastard!"

Rachel fell backward onto the floor. Being six months pregnant, she was not in the best of shape to restrain a girl who was already more than a match in size and strength. Gustavo tried to restrain Deborah from behind while she kicked Rachel where she lay. The other children started crying, the eldest sisters pleading for it all to stop. Gustavo managed to pin Deborah to the floor, but she fought back, her knee striking his ribs. As he moved off, Deborah rolled over and put a hard bite on his now-exposed lower ankle. Gustavo pushed her away. Deborah sprang to her feet and ran out of the house while Gustavo helped Rachel to her feet, and she, looking bewildered, looked down at Gustavo's ankle – it was bleeding from Deborah's bite.

Ioan drove to his apartment on River Road. He reached into his jacket pocket as his cell phone chimed up. It was Cecilia calling. Cecilia had been someone he had an ongoing love affair with for decades, but it was uniquely a nonsexual affair, though physical contact was always something they did for minutes or hours when time allowed.

"I need some help, Ioan: hot water heater went out again and I can't get the pilot to light. Neil promised when he bought the house, we would get a new water heater, but I am still waiting. Are you busy right now?"

"Sure, I will be right over, but get your air fresher out: I need a shower," Ioan explained.

Cecilia, a girl he had known since elementary school, had grown into a striking blonde beauty. He could never deny her any request. He was attracted to elfin features in childhood, falling in love with her quiet and reserved demeanor that always welcomed his attention. She was two years younger, and from the start, Ioan had a protective fascination with the little neighborhood girl. He would go four extra blocks to walk her home after school. Through the years, his feelings never waned through their separate maturations, distances most distant, and other romances. He went off to Flagstaff, and beyond, she moved to Houston. Now, they were neighbors again in the River Road ghetto. Married for a few short years, she had become someone's wife for a second time. Ioan told her long ago that her being happy with or without him was what he wanted most for her. Now, her second husband, Neil Davis, was an architect who had large contracts designing churches. She would have evenings with Ioan when they meet for dinner or have walked along the river when her husband was working into the evening, as her husband often worked late; at least, that was his explanation.

Presently crouching at the bottom of the hot water tank, Ioan pushed the red button as directed for ten seconds and poked the long stick-lit match into a small portal wherein the gas jet pilot flame grew into a deep to light blue teardrop flame.

"Okay, now I need to get cleaned up myself," Ioan stood up, dusting off his pants.

"Thank you, Ioan. Neil has been promising to replace that thing since we moved in. Get in the shower," Cecilia said, "Don't worry – he's away in Houston till tomorrow night."

Ioan did not want to stay the night. While the fantasy of making love to Cecilia all night seemed possible, he also did not want to complicate her life or his. Being able to spend some quiet holding time, even just her pinkie, was all the expressive enactment of their bond he ever wanted, as she had done so long ago in their childhood years. The loss of his internship did leave a feeling in need of any distraction and relief from anxiety about the future.

Out of the shower, he toweled off, wrapped himself in it, and noticed his clothes were missing. He found Cecilia in the hallway wearing her blue silk nightgown and his purple tie tied in a double Windsor around her throat. She carried the familiar scent of lavender and rosemary.

"They'll be done in a while. Cold water washing does not take long, but it will be another thirty minutes in the dryer. Go get in bed, under the covers. 'Baby, it's cold outside,'" Cecilia gently joked, slowly blinking her eyes like a cat.

Ioan did as she said remembering *it always starts this way, but I wonder if she ever really is aware of the deep feelings I have for her.* Cecilia aimed the remote at the bedroom television, and the screen lit up with a snow leopard climbing over a snow-patched rocky terrain to the barely audible narration of David Attenborough. Cecilia pulled back half the covers on the queen-sized bed and lay by Ioan's side. She reached for his hand and held it as they quietly gazed into the other's quiet face. For the first time, through all the times of mixed signals, of longing for connection, and confusing heart words of devotion, Ioan felt for her that at last she was reading him: *she really does feel my love.*

About an hour later, Ioan awoke. Cecilia was asleep next to him. He reached over quietly, loosening his tie from around her throat, and slowly pulled the ribbon silk from her without waking her. He found his clothes in the laundry room, dressed, and peeked back in on Cecilia, who was still sleeping quietly. *Adios, Angel. See you again soon,* he whispered soundlessly and left.

HOME OF ARTURO AND MARTHA CRUZ, ATTORNEYS AT LAW

"This all happened back in 2012," Arturo exclaimed, "and now they have convened a grand jury, and they found the mother is just as guilty as the father."

"If she was neglectful in reporting, sure, she's just as guilty, and if she ignored her daughter's outcry for months afterward, she is more than guilty," Martha replied with a certain calm elegance well practiced through her years of divorce court experience. "Are you going to defend her?"

"For $20,000? Of course. She has put the certified check in the mail today!" Arturo announced in his self-congratulatory tone. He wore the grinning expression of the cat that ate the canary.

"I read the OPD reports this morning while waiting around at the courthouse. He did it, and the mother is just too in love with him to believe her own daughter," Arturo pronounced with complete certainty. "I have read a dozen, no three dozen cases, just like this, and they all read the same: first they hug their victims, then they rub on their victims, and finally they start putting their hands inside their underwear. This guy is so typical: a stepfather with an obviously high libido. He and Rachel already had children before their marriage and four children together since they wed," Arturo explained.

"So, what has been happening that all this is only coming to court now?" Martha asked.

"The girl was found wandering out on I-10 back in 2012. When the OPD took her to their station, she claimed her stepfather had been sexually molesting her for months. CPS was notified, and they contacted her parents, recommending a safety plan. The next day, Mom went to the OPD and signed an agreement to separate from her husband and allow her daughter to go stay with her older adult sister," Arturo explained with his characteristic *I am always right even when I lie* vigor.

"And so, what was the hold-up? Why is it just coming to court now?" Martha asked.

"The kid was in therapy. It seems the therapists told CPS investigators they had doubts about the girl's outcry being believable. There were a lot of inconsistencies: she said he touched her every night for months, but then he was away for weeks at a time. He was off in Midland, which means some of the nights she accused him of abuse could not have happened. She had a special treatment session with a social worker doing some 'biofeedback' stuff, whatever that is, so anyway that therapist wrote that the girl admitted to dreaming up the sex abuse. I don't know, but the girl has some learning and emotional problems that have been ongoing for most of her life," Arturo expounded. "Anyway, she is a prime victim for grooming by a sexual predator. So, a few months back, the Crockett County Prosecutor convened a grand jury and indicted the stepfather, which she was satisfied with, but then the grand jury handed down a second indictment on the mother: four counts based on her neglecting to act against her husband and refusing to believe her daughter."

"So, what are you going to do? I mean, besides, go to Ozuna three times a month." Martha asked.

"I'm going to call the crazy Grecano Apostolos. There's too much psychobabble in the therapy reports. I need someone to second chair when it comes to jury selection.

And I need someone to deal with this woman. Every time I talk to Rachel on the phone, she goes off into 'all too much to be believed' conspiracy stuff about the Prosecutor, OPD, and the county courthouse staff being in league with her ex-husband's extended family, who all supposedly have ties to the Sonoran drug cartel, and how the whole county is involved in drug money laundering. I need a buffer between me and that stuff. Apostolos says he's a good listener, so I am going to get him to listen to all that crap. I don't need any of that shit!" Arturo exclaimed with frustrating agitation.

"Remember, I need Ioan to get the cats. Dorcas insists they are not to be flown over, and she is willing to pay to have them brought here," Martha cautioned, as she needed someone who would handle that feline delivery service with care and expedience. Martha's client, Dorcas, was a young adult who had been placed in a mental health clinic in Oxnard. Dorcas seemed to have had a psychotic episode while on the road to Texas, never making it further than Palm Springs, not the most direct route for her sojourn. Her pets had been placed in an animal shelter near Santa Barbara.

The cats had originally belonged to her partner, Kirsten, who suffered from major depression. While Dorcas was away for a week-long jewelry-making workshop in Quartzsite, Kirsten fell deeper into the gloom. She undressed one long, lonely afternoon, got into the bathtub and slashed her wrists. Days later, neighbors found her body, which the hungry cats had been eating. Dorcas was not shocked by what many would find gruesome. To her New Age thinking, Dorcas felt it made her closer to the cats as they had ingested not just Kirsten's flesh but her mystical body as well.

_________ MONDAY IN
SEPTEMBER, 2023

STEPPING INTO THE AIR OUTSIDE THE SANTA BARBARA Airport, Ioan immediately felt the embrace of fresh sixty-degree air with its mix of eucalyptus and sea breeze scents. He relished being back in Santa Barbara, where he once visited the Joseph Campbell Library at the Pacifica Institute. The memory of finding Campbell's copy of the Mahabharata bloomed as he searched for a suitable motel for the night's stay. When he opened the book fifteen years earlier, his eyes fell on the passage about Udishtara looking up at the night sky and seeing how the constellations had changed, signaling the end of this family's exile. *Is this a new beginning for me or just another approaching exile?* Ioan wandered.

After a comfortable night in a Best Western, Ioan sat

alone in Starbucks with a grande cup of Komodo dragon coffee as he looked over the Crocket County files Arturo's office had sent. The investigating officer, Cassandra Troianos, detailed the confused and confusing layout of finding Deborah wandering along the westbound I-10 highway in the dark new moon night. Troianos reported Deborah as being extremely guarded and minimally communicative in the glare of the OPD curser's bright lights. In the station house, she broke down and told Troianos she was a victim of sexual abuse by her stepfather. Deborah told Troianos that for months, he had been coming into her bedroom at night, laying himself down to spoon himself behind her and reach around fondling her body. *Who else in the home knew this was going on? Surely, the other children would have gotten some hints about it,* Ioan imagined.

Ioan sent off an email to his fraternal twin brother, Leonidas. He messaged Nidas (he hated being called "Leo") about losing his internship at Encino Groves. He laid the barest details of his present assignments for Martha and Arturo. He asked how their ninety-year-old father was doing in his new group home in Woodland Terrace. Together, they were brothers who fought against each other as often as they fiercely allied against perceived common threats, but they could only imagine denying their brotherhood. Imagining and intuiting were functions they both humbly applied to align their understandings.

After checking Google Maps and then over and over retracing his drives through the county roads of coastal California, Ioan found the animal shelter. At the counter he presented himself to the matronly pleasant receptionist, Margaret. She wore a blue smock with lighter blue cat patterns.

"This really so good of you to do this," Margaret said in a soft, soothing and happy voice. "Ithaca and Imbros have been good kitties. We will miss them."

Ioan thanked Margaret, letting her know her graciousness was appreciated. With the help of one of the shelter's attendants, Ioan loaded each cat into the pet carriers he had purchased at the local Petco. Once in the rented SUV, he positioned himself in the back seat overlooking the rear space where the carriers sat side by side. He unzipped each carrier and Ithaca, and then Imbros slowly raised their heads out.

Ioan spoke to them softly, blinking his eyes slowly to each of them, making the sort of feline eye contact they would appreciate.

Fearful of driving on the 101 Highway, Ioan found a route over the coastal mountain range that would take him to Bakersfield. It was a winding, up-and-down two-lane road descending into small vales and upwards to switchbacks above clouds. He had a running conversation with Imbros, who sounded almost human at times – obviously, he was protesting the ride. Ithaca found her way to the console and seemed to plead with Ioan to end their "abduction." "I know this is not easy for you two, but at the end of this trip, you will be in your new home with Dorcas," Ioan offered as consolation, a consolation he would make again and again as the three headed back to Texas.

_________ LATE AFTERNOON,
SEPTEMBER, 2023

RACHEL PULLED UP TO THE LAW OFFICE AFTER HER FIVE-hour drive to San Antonio. Arturo had weakly asked for a face-to-face meeting, though much of the reports, evaluations, and other legal documentation had been received and acknowledged. Arturo really dreaded the meeting, but Martha had strongly advised him that the interview was necessary for a case such as Rachel's. He needed to see Rachel's demeanor and how she presented herself.

Rachel was well-dressed and presented as a well-educated woman. She had been a BSN but had stopped working as a nurse after she divorced Deborah's father.

"We are Crypto-Jews. My mother received title to the motel property from Governor Perry as he recognized her, our family's Spanish Land Grant claim from King Philip II in the 1500s," Rachel explained as Arturo had been sitting down then getting up and pacing around his office. *Here it comes* – what he did not want to hear.

"We sold the property because these characters from across the border would show up and just hang out with that real molester, Josh, who had been having sex with Deborah," Rachel said with urgency in her voice. "They were all a part of what has been going on with the cartel and their money laundering in the county."

"Look, I can't do anything with that. We cannot use Deborah's sexual behavior in your defense," Arturo insisted with some agitation. "What is going on with persons known and unknown in the county is not my concern. I want to get you a 'not guilty' verdict, that's all!"

"But they are all in on it. Troianos is a sister-in-law of Lionel, Deborah's father. Josh is Troianos' cousin. Those Mexicans that showed up were bringing in contraband, buying guns, and were part of the kidnapping ring in Mexico," Rachel spoke up with consternation. "You've seen Man on Fire? I think Josh was the Voice here on this side of the border, for real! He was calling kidnap victim's families in Mexico to arrange ransom payments. After Josh disappeared, the FBI came and questioned us. That's when my mother and I decided to sell the motel property."

"So what? I can't do anything about that, and that is not what we are here for," Arturo complained. "None of that will help your case."

With frustration, Arturo dialed up Ioan, "What are you doing, Loco? I need you to talk to Rachel now!"

"Okay, I'm outside Bakersfield. Put her on Facetime. I want to ask her questions, too. [after a minute of transfer] Hello Rachel, I'm Ioan."

"Hi, Ioan, how are you?" Rachel asked with a pleasant smile.

"I'm good. I read through some of the papers you have sent. Forgive me for being straightforward about this, but your other children have never said or hinted about your husband's actions toward Deborah or themselves?"

"Gustavo has been a loved and loving father to all our children, Deborah included," Rachel responded with emotional vulnerability in her voice. "Our family has been caught up in a 'crossfire' between the county courthouse, the corrupt police department, and the county tax assessor."

"Arturo and I want to get you off; the charges against you dropped completely. I understand Gustavo has his own attorney, an experienced one, from what Arturo has told me. You may have another case with the county, but for now, we need to work together to get you cleared of all four counts against you," Ioan replied, trying to offer some consolation and support. "I get 'mad at the world' too when everyone seems to be 'out to get me.' Let's work together now and focus on the support for and of your family and the endgame that will be your exoneration in court."

"Okay...okay. Thank you, Ioan. I look forward to seeing you soon," Rachel said, sounding somewhat relieved.

Ioan had made it to Bakersfield at three pm local time. Ithaca and Imbros had quieted down but were stirring as he parked the car in a Panda Express parking lot. "I'm going to get my feed bag on, guys. I'm going to have to keep you in here. There's fresh water and more food for you," he told them as if they were his children.

Inside the Panda Express, waiting for his to-go order, Ioan started thinking about Gustavo. He tried to imagine what he looked like: was he a tall Apache-like Southwestern male like the ones he knew from his days in Arizona? *Natives may be prone to alcoholism and even huffing, but rarely was child sexual abuse something that was reported on the "Rez,"* he recalled.

Back on the road, Ioan drove on, hoping to make it to Kingman before dark. His half-eaten spicy beef and fired rice permeated the SUV's interior. Ithaca and Imbroz started to cry out again. "I know, guys, it's torture for you, but we'll find a room, and we can bed down quietly tonight," he said, trying to keep them attended to while he dialed through the radio signals, trying to find the classical music stations they had been listening to on the way to Bakersfield. There was nothing but Christian Rock and sermons. The landscape was now the crumpled ochre desert terrain of past earthquakes and distant hills with giant wind turbines.

As the sky darkened, they were now on the outskirts of Barstow. It took a few missed turns, but Ioan found his way to Highway 40 East, the successor to the old Route 66. Finding a Travel Lodge, he offloaded the pet carriers and brought in their cat litter pan and other supplies. Placing the carriers on the extra bed, he unzipped each one. Ithaca and Imbroz jumped out. Imbroz went looking for a place to hide while Ithaca explored the room.

Ioan opened his laptop while the remains of his Panda Express meal heated up in the microwave. Having gone through the Crockett County reports, he turned his attention to what Rachel had sent Arturo's office about Deborah's therapeutic treatments. Early in her life,

Deborah had been diagnosed back in Cleveland, Texas, as being "bipolar." He had seen young children given this diagnosis when he worked as a clinical liaison in Phoenix in 2006. This seems as too strange now as it was then, he thought. *After all, a young child's sensorium is like a lantern shining on everything in their immediate environment – they are naturally ADHD until they start focusing on what they need and what fascinates them. The medical model is to medicate first and sort out treatment later!*

Ithaca jumped up from the bed next to Ioan. She came up to his head and poked her nose in his face. He reached over and stroked her shiny black coat. "Another day and night, and I will get you guys home." Ioan began to think of his passengers as having greater awareness of what was happening to them. Their fears and discomforts were becoming a little more tolerable for them. Their trust seemed perceivable as Imbroz jumped up on the bed to join Ithaca.

The next morning, Ioan heard his cell phone chime as he was getting out of the shower. After toweling off and getting dressed, he looked up at the caller. It was Leonidas, back in San Antonio.

"Que tal, Nidas-san, how's my one and only 'womb-mate'?" Ioan greeted as Leonidas answered.

"How's our 'cat whisperer' doing? Where are you today? How are the cats doing? They haven't eaten your legs yet, have they?" Leonidas asked, remembering what Ioan had told him about Kirsten's suicide.

"They have been very cooperative when it comes to loading them and not messing with the driver. But once we're moving, they doth protest way too much. Imbros almost sounds human at times," Ioan answered.

"What's with these island names for these cats?" Leonidas asked.

"Kirsten was an anthropologist, from what Martha told me about her. She studied ancient Koine Greek, specializing in reworking translations of the Iliad. How's Pop? Did you see him yesterday?"

"Pop is good. After last month's house key stealing and the other angry stuff I told you about, he is settling in. When I saw him yesterday, he wanted me to be sure to 'check in with your mother who is around here somewhere...' Two years now since her passing, and he still sees her, probably in his dreams. I took him to Starbucks again. He thought our mother made the coffee cake – he loved it. Amelia is taking good care of him. The woman is a living saint. This group home may not be the most upscale, but he is quite comfortable now. You chose this group home well, Hermano," Leonidas assured.

"Thank you, Nidas-san, I hope I did my best. Thank you(!) for all you have been doing for Pop while I'm out here on the road. I hope to be back in two days. I am leaving Barstow within the hour. I want to make it to Tucson before dark today."

"Be safe. Ve con Dios y odigeite process kai min epitakhynete [drive carefully and don't speed]," Leonidas farewelled.

"Your Greek is coming along! See you in a couple of days, Bro."

The drive was getting smoother for Ioan. The cats still protested loudly, and he responded to every utterance each one made. Ithaca was becoming more vocal compared to yesterday. Imbros lay in the back with his body tucked into the rear flooring and backing of the rear passenger seats. Ithaca ducked under the front passenger seat. They settled down as Flagstaff's classical station of NAU became clearer with strains of Mozart. The sky was a brilliant blue with the white con trails of jetliner streaks.

Needles was cool and sunny as Ioan pulled into a Chevron. As he pumped gas into the SUV he thought about eating and thought he ought to keep going. Then he figured that the cats could use some motionless downtime, given he was determined to cross three-quarters of Arizona before sunset. As he turned to get back on I-40, he noticed Helen's Gyros, which looked like a converted Jack in Box just ahead of the access road. *Sure,* he thought, *Greeks are everywhere!* He pulled in and ordered a spicy gyro, Helen's special of the day. As he sat on one of the outdoor picnic benches, he opened his laptop and found a new attachment of documents Arturo's office had sent.

Medical notes from one Usha Kohli, MD, stood out: as a preschooler in Cleveland (TX), Deborah had been recruited into sexual behavior with another little girl at daycare. *This seems like she was left alone, or at least not attended to enough, and emotionally neglected. She found, or was found, by someone who was "adrift" in the same lonely "boat." Interacting with another child who was molested before she even understood or cared whether it was proper seemed to feed Deborah's longing for human connection at an early age.*

_________ MID-WEEK IN
SEPTEMBER, 2023

LEONIDAS WOKE EARLY THE NEXT DAY. THE MORNING SUN softly filtered through the trees as he drove down Melrose on his way to Woodlawn Terrace to pick up his father, Dimitrakis.

"I had breakfast. You should try Amelia's migas – they're really tasty!" his father announced.

"Well, how about a second cup of Starbucks coffee, Pop?"

"Yeah, sure, let's go. Adios, Amelia," Dimitrakis called out as he followed Leonidas out the door.

Leonidas was happy his father had adjusted so well to

living in the group home. *He still misses Julia so much, but at least he's become calmer about it,* Leonidas thought with mixed feelings of gratitude and grief.

The midtown drive wound through Olmos Park to the parkway below the Olmos Dam. Leonidas remembered when he and Ioan rode their bicycles across the top of the dam: *that was a wonderful childhood we had. Dee and Julia really were good parents.*

"Look at the forest!" Dimitrakis exclaimed as he marveled at the thick tree growth in the Basin. The Basin side of the dam had been a shallow lake decades ago. There were still some long dried-up ponds to be found there.

"Remember when Dahlia got lost back there?" Dimitrakis asked. *Wow! He remembers that! It's been fifty years, at least. Is it the scent of something in the air?* Leonidas wondered, giving his father a look of wonderment.

Dahlia was Julia's young cousin from their grandparents' hometown in Asherton. Leonidas had always held a special place in his heart for her. She was five years older and had come to live with his family at the end of her high school years. Dahlia and her father, Emilio, had had a troubled relationship from the start. Emilio Zabaleta returned from the Vietnam War after serving as the cook on the USS Maddox. He was regarded as a promising young veteran with big plans for starting an upscale Tex-Mex resturaunt chain. He was looking forward to rejoining his wife Linda, who was then ready to give birth to their first child, the son that would make Emilio proud and show his siblings and extended family what a virile man he was. The birth of Dahlia was a great disappointment, and he refused to go to the hospital to see his newborn daughter.

Emilio's hard-hearted feelings towards his daughter continued into her early and middle childhood. Dahlia, at heart, was a gregarious, alpha personality like her father. Dahlia was mistreated harshly by Emilio whenever he felt situations warranted punishment, severe punishments: locking her in a closet, humiliating her in public, or just ignoring her when she clearly needed his help.

Dahlia demonstrated literary talent early in life. She wrote short stories and poetry in elementary school. In junior high, as the sixties rolled into various tragedies, the Kennedy and MLK assassinations, Dahlia began drinking alcohol covertly and experimenting with drugs. During these years, Ioan and Leonidas began to consider Dahlia as someone very special in the extended family. In high school, she had her writings published in the San Antonio Light. Leonidas felt a strong and loving connection to

Dahlia, and she would reciprocate by having soirees when time allowed. But it was not all clean fun.

Dahlia was careful about keeping Ioan and Leonidas away from her addictive behavior. After she graduated from high school, she moved in with her high school English teacher and enrolled in St. Philip's College. Professors lauded her work, and her drug use became just as profound. One afternoon, she was arrested outside Frost Brothers for shoplifting.

That evening, Julia was in inconsolable tears and filled with anger towards Emilio: he refused (once again) to go see Dahlia, this time in Bexar County Jail, nor would he seek legal remedy of any sort: "She needs to be punished and sitting in a cell for a few weeks should straighten her out...maybe!"

Dee and Nidas went to see Emilio. To Dimitrakis, Emilio repeated his tirade that Dahlia deserved to be in jail, "that useless junkie!" he exclaimed in response to Dee reminding him she was his daughter. Dee, feeling frustrated and ineffectual, stood up from the table and moved towards the door. Leonidas moved from the corner of the room and sat down directly across from Emilio.

"Dahlia has a drug problem, but that's because she

needs your help; she's always needed your help," Leonidas pleaded.

"Those kinds of people are weak! You're just a kid! What do you, Grecanos Locos, know about raising kids? Your parents couldn't straighten her out. She writes all that 'revolutionary,' hippie crap; the dumbass newspaper published it – so what!" Emilio responded vehemently.

"Dahlia is courageous – whether she's wrong or right. I see a lot of you in her," Nidas offered with a calm fear, knowing full well that he was just a high school student talking back to a man he had admired all his life.

Emilio leaned back in his chair, inhaling deeply while keeping a firm and angry gaze on Leonidas.

"That's enough, Nidas. Let's go," Dimitrakis said quietly, placing his hand on his son's shoulder. As they closed the door behind them, Linda tearfully knelt next to Emilio, "The boy is right – Dahlia needs our help. Please, Daddy, she's been in there for two weeks now. Let's bring our baby home."

CROSSING THE COLORADO RIVER, THE LANDSCAPE BECAME more rugged and rusted. *Todos en la Arizona es rojo!* Ioan remembered answering Leonidas when he asked how things were going when Ioan first moved out there twenty-five years ago. Kingman sprawled out along I-40. There were distant housing units clustered together, Ioan could see as he topped a rise on the highway. Ithaca and Imbroz had been vocalizing their pleas for the unsettling motion of the drive to stop. "Somewhere over there is the site of the second flying saucer crash of 1947," Ioan told his passengers. Imbros and Ithaca became silent. "You cats know something I don't?"

Finding the right turn off to state Route 93, Ioan

marveled at how the high red stone formations looked like eroded temples and ancient fortress structures of some long-vanished builders. The vulcanism of past eruptions beautifully cluttered the landscape, with yucca and ocotillo sprouting out between the rocky outcroppings.

As Ioan approached Wickenburg, the traffic became an unexpected crush. Years ago, Ioan had responded to a job offer to work in a rehab clinic in Wickenburg. He learned during the phone interview that some well-known actors had gone there for treatment. Far from Los Angeles and out-of-state, it was a great place if one wanted to disappear from the spotlights of *Access Hollywood* and reporters of the *National Inquirer*. Now, the highway was clogged with traffic as Wickenburg's roadways were under new miles of construction. The SUV's gas was down a third of a tank. It would make it to Phoenix, but Ioan considered that it was time for a shortstop.

Lucha's was a side-of-the-road souvenir shop and gas station on the southern end of Wickenburg. Ioan, topped off the tank, checked on the cats, who were quiet and seemed too stressed to raise their heads as he spoke to them. "We're going to take about fifteen minutes here, kids. I'll see if there are any turquoise collars in your sizes," Ioan joked.

Finding a park bench and table outside, Ioan opened a nectarine peach Red Bull and his laptop. There was another document waiting to be downloaded from Arturo's office. It was another layout from Rachel. She explained that Deborah's life with Lionel was full of mysteries and inappropriate handling of her personal hygiene. According to reports from Dr. Kohli, Deborah as a toddler often accompanied Lionel into public restrooms, Men's restrooms. Rachel found out that in the fourth grade, Deborah had attacked Lionel's mother one weekend when she stayed with her for the day. Two years later, soon after Deborah came to live with Gustavo, Rachel, and the other children, she became violent with Juan Carlos, Gustavo's son from his former marriage, as he laughed at Deborah for not believing she had lost a card game. Being older and taller, she pushed the little boy out of his chair, pinned him down, and slammed his head on the Talavera floor. Juan Carlos was taken to the hospital for treatment. There was another incidence of elder abuse by Deborah; this time, she assaulted Rachel's sixty-two-year-old mother, Esther. This happened two months after CPS investigations opened as Deborah was being placed with her maternal grandmother as part of her safety plan.

But what stood out the most was the answer to Rachel's

direct question to Deborah about the allegation of sexual abuse by Gustavo:

"Did Gustavo ever touch you inappropriately when you came to live with us?"

"You'll find out," Deborah responded cryptically.

It had been an uneventful day for Leonidas. After grading his sociology student assignments, he remembered Willie Nelson's admonishment: "Live every day as if it is your last, and one day you will be right." His phone lit up as it had been in silent mode. Leonidas answered his phone; it was Linda:

"Nidas, Emilio has expired," she said with somber relief. For the past five years, Emilio had several hospitalizations. He often had his lost his balance due to what appeared to be Parkinson's disease.

"I grieve with you for our loss. Is anything I can do?" Leonidas calmly asked.

"We will let you know. Dahlia is here. She's emotionally stable but a little under the weather health-wise. We are both struggling to stay healthy, but we are grateful that Emilio's long-suffering has ended," Linda explained in the quietly elegant voice she was well known for.

"We want you and Ioan to join our Asherton cousins, Charlie and Polo, to be pallbearers. The funeral will be next Thursday," she asked, "And Leonidas, don't tell your father, please. I want him to stay happy and not decompensate over Emilio's passing," Linda urged, her voice sounding anxious.

"Well, okay. Yes, it will be my honor to serve as a pallbearer. Ioan is out of town right now, but he should be back by next week," Leonidas answered, "Don't hesitate to call if there's anything I can help you all with."

Leonidas closed his laptop. Looking up the clock it was half past noon. *Dee ought to be finishing lunch. It's a good time for us to go to Starbucks.*

Arriving at the group home, Leonidas found his father sitting quietly in his room.

"How are things going today, Pop?" Leonidas asked in a cheerful voice.

"Emilio came by last night. He drove me over to Paseo Encinal," Dimitrakis spoke quietly. Emilio stopped driving ten years ago. Emilio's and Linda's home on Paseo Encinal was about a hundred years old. It was a large two-story rock-walled structure. Its spacious rooms had Persian rugs and large modern art paintings Emilio had done in a Mondrian style.

"He told me to take a last look around because he has decided to sell the property," Dimitrakis said with some sadness in his voice.

He *knows*. Leonidas recognized how prescient his father was even in his dementia.

THE LARGE MOUNTAIN FORMATIONS BEGAN TO RECEDE BEHIND him as Ioan reached the turn off to state highway 60 that would flow into I-10 just outside Phoenix. The sunlight was brightly glaring as the blacktop road glistened with shimmering heat. *Getting through Phoenix on I-10 is going to be quite the crush* Ioan imagined. Imbroz and Ithaca had been quiet for most of the afternoon drive since their stop at Lucha's.

Everything was completely different from what he had remembered from his last time there in 2008. The west side of Phoenix had sprawled out with row after row of strip centers, many of them with vacant retail spaces for rent. *Had they ever been occupied? Or were they the "graves" of businesses gone under, under the weight of the COVID pandemic?*

Ioan wandered as he stopped at traffic lights. The traffic was heavier now as he approached I-10, and traffic lights seemed completely ill-timed, timed, backing up traffic for mile after mile.

"Finally, we are getting to I-10," Ioan told the cats. The traffic was heavy but moving. "If we keep moving at 50mph, we could be in Tucson before sundown," Ioan announced as the traffic flow alternated between 50 to 65 mph, paralleling the dry Salt River bed. The drive past Mesa was flanked by many new strip centers. Most of them were vacant. I-10 south of Mesa became crowded at times, slowing speeds down to 40 mph. As Tucson neared, the traffic began to crawl. The cats began to stir and meekly cry out. "Yes, my friends were almost there!" Ioan told them with some relief, "We will find a nice big bed tonight." Ioan's eyeballs ached as floaters and streamers glided through his vision of passing cars and row after row of abandoned strip centers that lined the interstate.

"LEONIDAS, PLEASE, COME SEE ME. WE NEED TO TALK." IT was a text message Leonidas had not expected. *Why now? She banished me after I told her the divorce was as much her undoing as Stephen's. And is this really her?* Dahlia had been avoiding him and openly turning her back on him in public whenever they came within sight of one another. Her poetry had opened and closed their relationship rather prophetically long ago:

Two stray cats catch each other eyes.
Startled by the other, alerted and fascinated.
There is no knowing one would be around the corner.
Their eyes fixed on the other's sleek black form.

The poem was a confession about the incestuous union

Leonidas had been unsure about from its possibility. Dahlia was older by nine years. *As Freud said, a promiscuous woman is a person with "daddy issues,"* Leonidas recalled. Dahlia and Stephen's marriage was a "second time around" for both of the them. Their deal was that Dahlia, with her growing income from her publications and work for the Regional Behavioral Health Authority, establishing writing workshops for minors in the system, would support Stephen while he attended medical school. Upon graduation, Stephen revealed his new love relationship in a "Dear Joan" letter to Dahlia. She fell into a deep depression. She emptied her medication prescription bottles and downed as many of the "dolls" as she could with a tumbler full of Merlot.

"Have you talked to Dahlia today," Roger asked.

"Not today. She said she was going to spend time with Frida this afternoon," Leonidas answered, wondering if it was indeed the case.

Roger phoned Frida with his usual calmness. Roger had been a longtime confidant of Dahlia's with high literary expertise that made him a close friend of Ioan's and Leonidas' as well.

"Frida says Dahlia was supposed to be here with us!"

Roger announced with uncharacteristic anxiousness in his voice.

Leonidas arrived at Dahlia's. The screen door latch was quickly undone with his pocket knife. The locked door took a few tries with his plastic Discover card. The door opened, but the chain was in place. His arm did fit through the space. Using his pocket knife, he angled it so he could fit its point into the screws of the holding plate. For five frenzied minutes, he worked unscrewing the plate. He found Dahlia on her bed, completely unconscious, with a weak but slow pulse. He called 911 and waited. "Please, Dahlia, come back to us! The world still needs you," he said silently with urgency.

THE EASTBOUND I-10 TRAFFIC STARTED TO SPREAD OUT AS
Ioan drove through the outskirts of Tucson. The late afternoon sky was ablaze with the vibrant pink of the coming
Arizona sunset. Ioan recognized buildings along the
highway as he had seen them from fifteen years earlier.
How different that was from the new abandoned shop
boxes that had been thrown up along the interstate.
Stockham, Grant, and Speedway – the exits became immediately knowable as when he had returned from Phoenix
every day in years past. He looked over the possible motels
along the highway while trying to position for a smooth
exit onto an optimal offramp. Turning eastward towards
downtown Tucson, Ioan spotted the Best Western on North
Stone. *That will work out just fine. Divine Angels, I thank you
for guiding me to this comforting place of relief.*

"Island cats, we have found our safe harbor for the night!" Ioan settled into a comfortable room with a large king-size bed. He opened his laptop and started looking over the narratives concerning Dahlia's therapy sessions. Her bio-feedback sessions seem to reflect her improvement. The therapist was quoted telling Deborah her incidences of being sexually abused may not have been real: "The brain does not sleep but actively 're-processes' your memories. Your recent results show an improvement from when we started a few weeks ago."

"You mean I may have dreamed Gustavo was touching me?" Deborah asked.

"Only you know for sure, but given some of the inconsistencies you have given about it, things fit the 'improbable' way dreams happen," the therapist answered.

Throughout the night, Ithaca and Imbroz ran around the room as if playing tag with each other. Ithaca would jump up on the bed, approaching Ioan for attention. Imbroz followed, only to be swatted claws-in by Ithaca. "Come back, Imbroz, let me see you," Ioan called out, but he slipped away under the king-size bed.

Ioan dozed back into sleep and *made it in three hours*

flat. The early morning traffic in Houston was really light today. The Washington Heights neighborhood was still in the soft, foggy morning light. *I wonder if Cecilia is up yet?* Presently, Ioan begins to knock but is distracted by a tuxedo/Sylvester car that brushes up against his leg. *Where did you come from?* The cat stared up at Ioan and winked his right eye. It was a signal! *I'm dreaming. So, I can just go in.* Entering the front room, Ioan could see Cecilia lying in bed through the French doors to her bedroom. *Cecilia, I'm here. Should I come back later? No response. Cecilia? Are you alright?* He approached the edge of her bed. Cecilia lay there completely still.

The image of Cecilia remained in Ioan's inner vision as he began waking up to one of the other cats jumping up on the bed. As his awareness of wakefulness took hold, Ioan got up and showered. Laying in the bathtub, he relaxed, assured that the cats would not come near. After having the complimentary breakfast in the 1960s style café, Ioan returned to the room and began cleaning up fur balls and packing things up. Ithaca and Imbroz crouched under the bed in anticipation of being placed back into their carriers. Ithaca reluctantly allowed Ioan to haul her out from under the bed frame and compliantly place her in the first carrier.

Looking under the bed, Ioan was amazed that Imbroz was not there. *He must have gotten inside the box spring spaces.* Ioan removed the pillows and bedding, upended the mattress, and propped it against the drapes of the front window. The two box springs were then upended. *Where did he go?* Ioan looked behind the television, the chest of drawers below it, and under the furniture in the bathroom. He moved the mattress and looked behind the drapes. Frantically, he left the room, closed the door securely behind, and went to the lobby.

"I'm sorry to bother you about this," Ioan apologized to the concierge, "but one of the cats I brought is missing, and I have been very careful when leaving the room. Are there small panels, possible openings it could have squeezed through into one of the adjacent rooms?"

"Not that I know of, sir. You should speak to our house-maid. Would you like me to find her for you?"

A second stranger in the room might compound the problem. "No, I am going to give it another search. I am certain the cat did not get out the door, and all the windows have stayed closed. If I don't find him in the next hour, I will be back," Ioan gratefully replied.

Back in the room, Ioan began a systematic search from the front of the room, behind the drapes and mattress, to the displaced box spring halves, to the chest of drawers, to the bathroom. Frustrated, he made a call to Leonidas:

"It's like Imbroz is Schrödinger's cat! I am turning into a Harrison Ford character over here! He has completely disappeared to the point I am wondering if he ever was here!" Ioan explained with a frantic voice Leonidas knew quite well.

"Ioan-san, calm down. I understand you feel you might have let him out unknowingly, or he has found his way into some place in the room you have yet to look in, like maybe there's a loose vent or some way up into the ceiling space," Leonidas said in an even and relaxed tone. "Sit yourself down, if you aren't already, and stop looking for a moment since you have already looked in all the likely places. I know you want to be on the road now, but Imbroz will get hungry or need to relieve himself. He will appear out of his Schrödinger's quantum box, smile and all. If not, get the housemaid to help. Imbroz sounds like one slick cat to get by, my investigator brother."

"Imbroz has shown himself to be the more introverted of the two. Even when protesting, he sounds more human-like than just another meowing feline. Both these characters have shown some remarkable intelligence," Ioan said with some relief, feeling more at ease talking things out with Leonidas. "Thank you, Nidas-san. I am going to start in the back of the room and work my way to the front of the room. Take care. Tell Pop I am going to try to be back the day after tomorrow."

After searching the closet area where he had placed the litter tray, Ioan carefully turned around and looked under the counter/basin area. He opened the door of the bathroom, which he had closed before he left when he went to the lobby. Immediately, the toilet and bath looked empty, but there under the toilet tank, curled up securely, was Imbroz. *He must have been moving from hideaway to hide away every time I turned my back!* Imbroz appeared to have a "yeah, you caught me" expression and let Ioan pull him out and place him in his carrier. *I am two hours behind schedule now. Oh well, I will make some of it up on the New Mexico drive through Billy the Kid country, Land of Enchantment.*

_________ LATER, SATURDAY
AFTERNOON

LEONIDAS ARRIVED AT THE HOUSE ON AVANT. WALKING UP TO the door, he heard the faint melody of the piano next door: *Is that a record or Ralph Duran? It is Ralph playing Old Folks. I must be getting there myself to recognize it. Nobody plays those tunes anymore.* The open doors and windows of the neighborhood homes were showing the demographics of locals: elderly but active folks. It felt good to be in what, for the most part, is a forgotten enclave of the city. The weather was cooling from week to week but only a few degrees below 70 and then back up with the humidity of the cloudy sky that seemed poised to at least drizzle but never does.

Dahlia came to the screen door just as Leonidas turned to face the door and ring the doorbell.

"Here I am. How are you? Is Miriam here?"

"Come in. Come here." Dahlia urged, embracing him ardently, kissing on his neck as he held his head up cautiously straight. She wore a white Japanese-style robe with floral prints. A thin white scarf encircled her throat. She sounded as if she had just awakened.

"What's going on, Dahlia? Are you alright? Is Miriam here?" he asked as he stepped back while holding her forearms.

"Miriam left last month. She and I are no longer. Dancers! They love you madly till they decide they need cock! She's addicted to Tiago again for the 'first ten-hundredths time!" she bitterly exclaimed.

"Dahlia, poor Dahlia, you know you and I are not going through another tryst. We are too old and too well-schooled by each other. Will you ever give up this Ariadne complex, or is it going to be Gladys Garcia this time?"

"Neither! I asked you here because I need to know you will be good to me as I put things in order. I cannot stand going through chemotherapies again," she said with a harsh tone rarely heard from her sultry vocal cords.

"Dahlia, we all have cared for you: Dee, Julia, Ioan, and *myself too much, which is why I stayed away.* Especially after you became involved with Miriam, I felt that at last she would be happy, and you would have someone to give you the comfort and emotional support you deserved," Leonidas said, feeling his eyes welling up.

"Comfort? Support? From Miriam? She lives a fantasy of being the next Martha Graham! That's where she got the whole idea that sex with a man was necessary for becoming a great modern dancer. Sure, we were compatible in our vision of the arts and tastes in music, but once the 'magic' of being 'Dahlia Zabaleta's consort wore off, she could not make the reciprocal effort of allowing for my time with my writers and my readers, and she couldn't stand my criticisms of her literary attempts. So yes, I do feel like Ariadne again for another first time!"

Leonidas replied softly with a faltering voice: "Well, that blows my myth of your strong will and 'guiding thread to freedom from want, fear, and excess' you wrote about. I hate myself for triggering this unhappiness and all its discontent. You know, I have to thank Ioan for reminding me that one has to remember in these 'trigger' situations where the 'explosive complexes' are stored: in you, in me, in ourselves."

Dahlia slumped back in her chair: "Yes, 'St. Ioan full of degrees.' Your brother has always gone above and beyond like a Watcher, differentiating every human purpose under the heavens. You're a Chthonic angel, Nidas, but Ioan is the archangel. I loved you because you read me: my words, my Self, inside and out. Ioan was always, even as a boy, coldly analyzing everyone."

Leonidas approached Dahlia as she sat in her chair. He leaned forward, his forehead touching her forehead: "I am glad you called me. If there is anything you need to keep your content, please let me know. See you Friday at Mission Park to lay Emilio to rest?"

"Yes, Linda and the cousins will be there. Is Ioan coming?"

"I expect so. He made it with the cats to Tucson yesterday. Where's your new kitty, Dharma?" Ioan had found her one night near the old box cars near the railroad crossing at McCullough. These had been refitted as rental spaces, one of which Ioan and Leonidas had rented out for three months as rehearsal space for their musical pursuits. Dharma was a lovely little tuxedo kitten who walked up to Ioan, "asking" to be taken home. It was early August, and Ioan was not sure he could care for her, so he asked Dahlia if she would take her.

"The Cooper's hawk got her last week; at least, that seems to be her likely demise. It's a good death even for one so young: to be taken by a sky god."

Leonidas hugged Dahlia goodbye: "I will keep your 'thread' in hand, Ariadne, now and always."

＿＿＿＿＿＿＿ SATURDAY, LEAVING TUCSON

THE SKY BLAZED A BRIGHT BLUE AS THE RIBBON OF BLACKTOP I 10 rolled out eastward. Traffic was light and swift. Eastern Arizona is high and dry as it courses toward the Continental Divide in New Mexico. The jumble of red granite boulders that make up Texas Canyon came into view. Ioan remembered that long ago, the proposed territory of Arizona went from El Paso to San Diego, a dry desert strip below the latitude of 33 degrees. The cats remained quietly curled up next to each other in the back of the SUV. The radio broadcast of the University of Arizona KUAT piped out the Mahler Fourth. "It's a good day to be out on the road," Ioan told the cats, "even if you two would rather be hiding under a bed somewhere."

Crossing the state line the landscape lost its reddish

hue and turned a pale yellow as the landscape flattened out. KUAT faded away as the Rachmaninoff Second Concerto commenced. Ithaca made her way to the middle of the front seats, pleading for the trip to end. "Okay, Ithaca, I hear you. We will stop in Deming soon, just another ten miles," Ioan responded. Ithaca got off the console and crawled under the passenger seat. *She thinking:* *"what a mean guy" I am.*

Stopping in Las Cruces, Ioan fueled up the SUV as he stared up at the mid-afternoon sun. *I'm behind schedule, but I might make it to Del Rio by dark.* The weather was breezy with cloudy skies. *Once through El Paso, I believed the miles of I-10 to Hwy 90 would go by quickly.* But they wouldn't: I-10 was diverted to 375 as the interstate was being "reconstructed." Several hours would now be added as the "parking lot" traffic jammed into and out of El Paso. *Should I just stop here or try to make it to Ft. Stockton or maybe Alpine?* "What do you guys think?" he asked Imbroz and Ithaca. Their silence was encouraging for Ioan to continue the slow crawl to the outskirts of El Paso. Gone were the Pecan tree orchards he remembered from his 2008 trip. Now, there were gas stations, strip centers, and acres of other urban sprawls of storage units. El Paso was now a "Big City." Finally, as he left Horizon City suburb behind, did the familiar West Texas landscape of distant mountains and high desert surround the highway.

The crawl out of El Paso had been tiring. Ioan stopped in Sierra Blanca to "tank up" on a nectarine-flavored Red Bull. The sun was casting long shadows. Imborz and Ithaca were still and quiet as he looked in on them before getting back in the driver's seat. Less than an hour later, they were outside Van Horn and the exit to Hwy 90.

There was a Border Patrol checkpoint to go through. Ioan slowed to 10 mph as he entered the terminal, stopping right next to the BP officer: "Who's in there with you?" he asked in a mildly authoritarian voice, noticing there were small movements in the rear section of the SUV. "Just two black cats and they are not jazz musicians," Ioan replied. The officer smiled, "Get moving."

The stretch to Marfa and Alpine was empty Highway 90, with distant grey mountains beckoning towards the borderland. Reaching Marfa, the shadows cast darkly upon the roadway as now the mountains were closing in. Reaching Alpine, Ioan stopped to gas up and get another Red Bull. The young girl at the counter bid Ioan her usual "Have a nice day!" "I'll do my best," Ioan replied, opening the Red Bull can as he headed for the door.

The sun was now setting below the tall mountains. Back behind the wheel, Ioan wondered if a night drive was still in him: his eyes were not the eyes of 2008, but 90 had been bereft of traffic. As he drove through Marathon, he thought of finding the one motel he remembered seeing from Amtrak years before. In the vanishing light, he looked for the features of the "Plain of Marathon" Captain Shepard of the 1881 US Cavalry had seen when he named the locale: as a youth, he visited the ancient site with his ambassador father. The West Texas landscape had the same features as Shepard had seen in Greece. *I am driving southeastwards. The Athenians charged southeastward to face Darius' forces centuries ago, towards the sea.*

"According to his text, Ioan made it from Barstow to Tucson," Martha told Arturo, "That's some hard driving. You said he never uses cruise control?"

"Yeah. That dumbass Grecano has a lead foot at the other end of his hard head!" Arturo quipped, downing the last half of his blue curacao cocktail. "Gimme some more of this."

"So, he could get here tomorrow. When do you need to be back in the Ozuna courthouse? Monday morning?" Martha asked, getting the glass pitcher from the counter.

"I need Apostolos with me for that. The ADA wants to

sit down with Rachel. She wants to offer a deal for her testimony against Gustavo."

"What difference will Ioan make for that? After all, it's the wife/husband betrayal 'under the bus' move. You think she's ready to do that after all these years of 'standing by her man?'" Martha asked critically, holding the glass pitcher of blue double alcohol drink.

"I don't care! That's why I want that crazy Grecano there so he can talk her into it. I just want to get this stupid thing over! Gustavo did it! He did it for months in 2012, and if Rachel is too 'blinded by love,' Apostolos can manipulate her into caring about her other six children's future. That delusional bitch Rachel and her 'crypto-kike' mother are rich enough to keep this thing going, but I want it done and off my plate!" Arturo vehemently insisted with impatience, "Come on, woman, pour me another."

"Tone down the dyspepsia, my dear. I want you to be done with all this, too," Martha replied as she filled his waiting glass with more of the blue curacao cocktail.

"All that bullshit about all of Crockett County being out to get their family is just that. I just want to get her off! Get her off any way that works!" Arturo insisted with impatience.

"Come on, Arturo: this is Red State Texas out there, and like Ioan said - just because she is paranoid does not dismiss the probability that some people out there have not had it in for them," Martha replied calmly, "It seems the ADA wants your help too, so that's a good thing. Get out there and close the deal Monday."

IOAN EYES BEGAN TO ACHE. HE COULD FEEL THE FATIGUE setting in. Imbroz and Ithaca had been quiet since Marathon. *I don't think I can make it to Del Rio. I wonder if I can find an open motel in Sanderson?* He recalled the washed out look of Sanderson from his Amtrak rides. He remembered seeing new café spots from the train during its brief stop there, but that was before COVID. As Hwy 90 curved into the Sanderson city limits, Ioan found a motel laid out across from the lit-up gas station/truck stop on his right. Taking the left turn into the parking lot, he parked before the front office door. The establishment was a typical roadside Texas cinder block motel in a squared "C" configuration, rooms one after the other with breezeways at the two corners of its formation. The locked office looked empty from its front casement window, but inside lights were on.

Ioan rang the doorbell but could not tell if it worked, so he pounded on the door. The sleepy, unkempt concierge entered the office from an inner door.

After securing a room in the center of the "C" formation, Ioan offloaded his luggage, the cat's amenities, and the cats. He poured fresh water into their bowls and laid out more food for each. He placed their litter box in the walk-in shower and inspected the room for all the possible hiding places the cats might get into. Imbroz jumped up on the bed right out of his travel bag– *that's not your usual move, or are you getting used to the rigors of our travels?*

Opening his laptop, Ioan began reading through the files he had started reviewing in Tucson. He found a narrative about sessions Deborah had with Allison McKenzie, LPC. There was a tone of frustration throughout the reading. McKenzie had determined that Deborah had difficulties making healthy attachments beginning in early childhood, something that fit her history of inconsistent care during her years of separation from her mother. The narrative revealed a childhood history of sexual behaviors with other children. McKenzie believed she was a child sexual predator who would confess in one session about exploiting younger girls. But at the next session, she claimed she had been groomed by the same girls. McKenzie kicked her out of his group therapy sessions for her constant mendacity. *This girl is not unlike some of the guys I knew from the adolescent sex offenders group I co-facilitated back in the '90s. The boys rarely lied but would minimize their offenses or hold things back. We never kicked any of them out. She may have been even more aggressive and threatening than a Lillian Hellman child character.* The narrative closed with a note that McKenzie passed away during a surgical procedure in 2019.

THE DRIVE ALONG HWY 90 FROM SANDERSON TO SAN Antonio was just not quick enough for Ioan, but compared to the drive from Barstow to Tucson, it was much shorter and less stressful. Imbroz and Ithaca arrived in their new cottage bedroom, still wary of staying out the open, quickly ducking into hiding places upon their release from their carriers. "You guys are in your new home now!" Ioan announced, "No more road life anymore."

Arriving at Martha's, Ioan was congratulated for accomplishing the errand from California in five days, with both cats delivered to their final destination. Arturo abruptly entered the room and, without even saying a 'hello, how are you?' urgently announced:

"We are leaving at 5 tomorrow morning. We need to be in Ozuna at 9 to meet with Pat Ripley," Arturo insisted.

"Pat Ripley?"

"She's the Ozuna D.A. She wants to offer Rachel a deal: if she testifies for the prosecution of Gustavo, Ripely will drop the four counts against her," Arturo answered with some relief in his voice.

In the dark of the early Monday morning, Ioan was behind the wheel again, this time driving Arturo out of San Antonio, heading northwest up I-10 – *God! How I hate I-10* – as the sixteen-wheeler freight trucks rumbled alongside Arturo's pickup truck.

"Watch your speed! DPS will stop us. We got to be at the courthouse by nine! We don't have time to stop for the cops," Arturo directed with angry fear.

"Please, Arturo, we are only doing 75 going downhill. I want to stay away from the sixteen-wheelers," Ioan replied, trying to calm down Arturo's stressful demeanor. "So why does the DA want to plead down Rachael's charges? Isn't she confident in her case that Gustavo is guilty?"

"He is guilty!" Arturo responded emphatically. "Ripley wants to recruit Rachael into the 'protect your daughter' corner, and for that matter, your other two girls, from Gustavo. I want you to tell her that her family's safety depends on cooperating with Ripley. You need to convince her so we can go home tomorrow and not spend all week in Ozuna."

"You know, I read through McKenizie's 'report,' that is, what Rachael sent us about his counseling Deborah. Did you read it?" Ioan asked, thinking, *was that not telling us about Deborah's mental condition, her impulsive and explosive behaviors(?).*

"I read all that stuff," Arturo resolutely pronounced. "So the kid was a brat – that's typical of the kind of little girl these guys groom." *Ioan just reads too much. These counselor types are so naïve when it comes to child abusers. I think he really likes Rachael too much to think she allowed Gustavo to molest Deborah,* Arturo told himself.

Arriving at the county courthouse, Rachael and her family, including Gustavo, Rachael's sister Sarah, and their mother Esther, along with Rachael's two young daughters, Miriam and Vanessa, their son Jacob, and Gustavo's son Juan Carlos, were all introduced to Ioan. They were all arrayed in their "Sunday best," looking more like a graduation party than a family with parents facing criminal charges.

Gustavo was not the tall or even medium-sized figure Ioan had imagined. He was five feet four inches tall and was wearing a clean, pressed white shirt, kaki dress slacks, a double Windsor purple tie, and a white yarmulke. *A yarmulke? How's that going to be received in court after the October 7th Hamas attacks in Israel?* Ioan wondered.

While the family members greeted Ioan as if it was a festive occasion, the two older sisters gave Ioan light hugs upon their introduction, and Gustavo remained guarded and pensive. Ioan was not sure what to say to him but was impressed with Gustavo's confident handshake. *There's something sincere and authentic about this guy,* Ioan thought as he looked into his unblinking eyes. Gustavo's expression was mixed with noble sadness and grateful contentment that his family was there with him. The two older sisters told Ioan that Deborah had been disturbing the family peace since her return to their mother. Esther and Sarah agreed as Juan Carlos showed Ioan the scar beneath his hair on the back of his stitched head injury suffered when Deborah assaulted him years ago.

Pat Ripley called Arturo from the hallway: it was time to sit down with Rachel and lay out terms for the removal of charges against her. Ioan noticed Vanessa motioning to him to come closer, "She's lying," she said softly so only he could hear her. Before Ioan could ask what she meant, he felt Arturo grab his arm, "Come on. I want you in on this 'sausage making.'"

With Rachel seated across from Ripley, Arturo introduced everyone to set his client at ease with what was about to come. Ripley placed down on the table a signed affidavit Rachel had agreed to back in 2012. It was her signed compliance with the county sheriff that Gustavo would move out of the home until the county court determined the safety of all minors in the home was verified by CPS investigators.

"Since you agreed to this, you admitted that there was a threat to the safety of your children. Your attesting to this document in court for the prosecution will clear you of all four counts of sexual abuse complicity in Gustavo's case," Pat Ripley calmly explained.

"But you know Deborah's accusations are hard to believe - just look at her mental health interventions," Rachel exclaimed with urgency.

"Yes, I have read her treatment documentation. I am

aware that she was diagnosed as being bipolar at age 7," Ripley responded calmly.

"If I may," Ioan introjected, "bipolar diagnosis of young children is a controversial practice that only few diagnosticians agree with. Something I have had some experience with and have doubted the validity of it."

"Well, sure. That is true in my experience as well," Ripley replied tersely. *She's got something going on with that,* Ioan thought; *why else would she have brought up the victim's mental disorder if she did not have some reason for doing so?*

Ripley pushed back from the table, offering, "Think it over. Talk with Counselor Arturo and Mr. Apostolos. Let me know what you decide. The courthouse opens at 8. Can we meet at 8:30?"

With the prosecutor out of the room, Ioan looked compassionately at Rachel, asking, "You understand that Ripley's offer will mean you will be a witness for the prosecution, so the charges against you will be dropped completely?"

Rachel cupped her face in her hands, tearfully crying, "I can't testify against Gustavo!"

"I understand your grief about this because you not only are devoted to your husband, but you don't believe anything of sort of sexual molestation happened to Deborah," Ioan said. *She's imagining how the imprisonment of Gustavo will be a death sentence for him, either by inmates or his eventual suicide after numerous beatings.*

"Look, we could get you out of this tomorrow!" Arturo insisted.

"She needs to consider this for herself, Arturo. What say we get an early lunch and let Rachel be with her family and talk things over with them?" Ioan suggested.

THE HEARSE PULLED UP TO THE FRESHLY OPENED GRAVE SITE. Leonidas waved to Linda and Dahlia, seated under the tent, looking stoic and strangely beautiful side by side. Leonidas joined his fellow pallbearers in anticipation of unloading Emilio's coffin. Cousin Nat rushed up to complete the cadre opposite Leonidas. He was called upon that morning to replace Ioan. Leonidas had not seen Nat for close to a decade. He remembered him as being about 5'9" and a fit marital arts practitioner. Now he seemed to be 5'6", several pounds over-weight, and seemed to be uncomfortable in his gray suit and wing-tip shoes. As the coffin was rolled out, each pallbearer passed the side handles on to the next handler in line until the full weight of the load was distributed to the three pairs of handlers. As they turned to carry the coffin to the grave, Nat seemed to lose his footing and lost his grip. Before the coffin could hit the ground, Leonidas got behind the load supporting it from beneath its underside. Nat had stopped himself from falling over completely.

"It's okay, Nat. Just walk alongside. We got it," Leonidas said.

"Gee, I am really sorry about that. These shoes are not what I am used to," Nat said with a sheepish grin.

With the casket in place, the celebrant began his eulogy and burial rite prayers; Leonidas recalled the Orthodox last words for the departed: "*Forgive his sins voluntary and involuntary of our father who has fallen asleep.*"

Once the cleric finished his service, Linda produced a bottle of Anejo Bacardi rum and a dozen small plastic glasses. Each extended family member was given a shot of the liquor, and Linda simply toasted it. "Here's to you, Emilio." She took a small sip and poured the remaining rum into his open grave. With the exception of Nat, who downed his drink, everyone present followed Linda's example. Dahlia simply pressed the rim of the glass to her lips and emptied all her rum into the casket.

Leonidas waited in the small line of relatives that formed up to express personal condolences to Linda and Dahlia. "The last always come first," Linda said as she accepted his sympathetic hug, "Come walk me to the car."

"Dahlia told me you came to see her last week," Linda spoke up with what sounded like a disapproving tone.

"Yes, she messaged me and asked me…"

"I know," Linda interrupted. "What she did not tell you is that we are both approaching the end of our days."

"We all are, every day we wake up…"

"No, Leonidas. You are always the 'glass half full' type, even as the 'well dries up.' Dahlia needs a new liver. I may not make it to next Summer, according to my oncologist. I want to watch over Dahlia after I am gone, but keep it…"

"You needn't say it," Leonidas assured her. "She and I already have made clear that we have a new and more loving relationship of the spiritual kind. Our 'close encounters' are now about emotional support and are not physical."

Leonidas looked Linda directly into her eyes. "We all need you and Dahlia. All the time we have left is so much more valuable than any of the past."

Linda half smiled saying, "Thank you," as she folded his hand in her hands, her eyelids closed.

RACHEL, ARTURO, AND IOAN SAT WAITING AROUND THE TABLE for Ripley to join them. Rachel was visibly stressed. *Doesn't she get it? We could all be done with this now!* Arturo thought, feeling frustrated by the DA keeping them waiting.

"I won't do it!" Rachel exclaimed. "I cannot testify against Gustavo."

"Yes, I understand a little about how difficult this is for you, Rachel," Ioan empathized. "All that is involved here is that you affirm your compliance – yes, with your family's enemies – but that your signature shows you were willing to follow the Law. Doing that can set you free to support Gustavo's case. Joe Rodriguez..."

"That's Jesse Rodriguez. His twin brother died last year," Arturo interrupted.

"Counselor Rodriguez can cross-examine you. That could be a 'Jack McCoy' opening for the truth about Deborah's accusation, or at least weaken the State's case against Gustavo," Ioan said with brightened enthusiasm.

Rachel pulled out a tissue to dry her eyes. She said nothing and looked up towards the ceiling. *Damn! We are going to be out here all week or even have to come back next week if Rachel goes to trial,* Arturo thought, looking down at the floor.

A quick knock at the door startled Rachel. The door swung open, and Ripley entered the room. "Good morning! Sorry to keep you waiting. I have been in the chamber with Judge Cardenas and Mr. Rodriguez. We won't need her testimony, and because she considered the offer, we are going to drop all counts against Rachel. So, that's it. Got to go ready for court."

The trial of Gustavo Philipe Alessandro began promptly at 10 am. Behind the prosecutor's table sat a middle-aged blonde-haired woman dressed in casual business attire. Behind the defense table, Gustavo's children sat together, all dressed in their "Sunday best" again. Further back, Rachel's sister, Sarah, wearing high fashion attire and very intense stare at the Judge and Ripley as they spoke. She was noticeable as she sat alone in the middle of the gallery of mostly empty seats. She would be Rachel's eyes and ears since Rachel had been ordered to stay out of the trial proceedings until called (that was now unchanged, though her legal disposition had changed). Jury selection was done fairly quickly with no refusals, with three Anglo men, three Hispanic males, and six Hispanic women.

Judge Cardenas then directed an inquiry to Gustavo's attorney: "Are those young people seated in the gallery behind you the defendant's children?"

"Yes, your Honor," Rodriguez softly responded.

"You said they are?" Cardenas asked with a louder authoritarian tone.

Leaning into his table microphone, Rodriguez repeated, "Yes, your Honor."

Gustavo might as well cop to a plea now, Arturo thought as he sat checking out the courtroom from a seat in the back row of the gallery; *Rodriguez is going to lose this one by sundown.*

"They all need to leave the court now so we can proceed to testimony," Cardenas ordered, "Ms. Ripley, once the children have left the court, call your first witness."

Pat Ripley stood up, turning her head so she could see Gustavo's children leave the court. She then announced, "Your Honor, the prosecution calls Deborah Grijalva."

Deborah emerged from a side door at the back of the court. She was well dressed, wearing big thick-rimmed glasses. Aside from the glasses she looked very much like a younger version of Rachel. Walking slowly and appearing unsteady, she stepped up to the witness platform.

"I do," Deborah responded weakly to the oath of testimony.

"Please, speak up," Judge Cardenas coolly demanded, "Every one of our jurors needs to hear you.
clearly."

"Ye-yess, sir. I do." Deborah responded with some trep-idation.

Ripley proceeded with the cursory clarifications: statement of witness' name, identification of Gustavo as stepfather.

Her outcry status and her current residence in New Mexico with her husband followed (who was curiously absent). Deborah then identified Gustavo as her perpetrator by pointing her finger toward the defense table without moving her head in Gustavo's direction.

"When did the defendant first molest you, and in what manner and where did he touch you?" Ripley asked.

"I remember it was the end of April. My sisters and I were getting ready for bed. He came into our room and hugged each of us. He hugged me longer than the others," she answered.

"What happened after that?" Ripley asked.

"He left and then came back."

"Right away?"

"No, it was like maybe an hour later, but I am not sure cause he woke me up."

"How did he wake you up?"

"I felt him get on the bed with me, behind me."

"So, you were on your side?"

"Yes."

"On your right or left side?"

Ripley is good, Arturo observed; *she wants exact details to avoid any chance of a miss trial.*

Ripley's questioning continued for two hours, extracting every detail:

"What were you wearing when Gustavo was groping you over your clothes? When did he start reaching under your pajamas? What did he say when he was fondling your breasts? Did he palm your vulva? Did he insert his finger?" For every occasion Deborah said Gustavo was to have molested her, Ripley asked for multiple detailed actions. Ioan observed the jurors being somewhat disgusted in their facial reactions to becoming more desensitized to Deborah's detailed responses to Ripley's questions as testimony went on. More yawns were evidenced as Deborah's answers became repetitively redundant and predictable.

Jesse Rodriguez then began his cross-examination of Deborah with a soft greeting and introduction of himself. He then asked his questions.

"In May of 2009, you visited your father's mother for the afternoon. Did you have an argument with her and hit her repeatedly with a ping-pong paddle?" Rodriguez asked in a rather gentle voice.

"I don't, don't re-remember..." Deborah replied rather blankly.

"Okay," Rodriguez replied calmly. "In July of 2012, you were at your grandmother's house in El Paso for a weekend visit. Do you remember punching her and then knocking over your grandfather when he tried to hold you back from hitting your grandmother again?"

"No, I don't remember."

"Do you remember hitting your stepfather and kicking your mother in August of 2012?"

"Ye...yess," Deborah answered weakly.

"Where did he get all this?" Arturo whispered to Ioan, who was sitting next to him.

"It was all in the email attachments and El Paso County report papers Rachel sent us." Ioan realized that either Arturo never read the cache of material or simply scanned it and forgot it all with his certainty of Gustavo being guilty. *This is the stuff that reveals who Deborah really was at the time Gustavo was supposed to be molesting her. He's a small man, and she's not a small girl. He looks so sad there. He must feel helpless.*

The court recessed after the defense cross-examination.

"Ripley is going to win this thing," Arturo said with certainty, "Rodriguez is such a 'salchicha Florida.' There's no way he's going get a not guilty verdict."

"Did you watch the jury?" Ioan asked.

"Yeah, they're ready to put themselves and this trial to bed. Gustavo is going to get locked up, and none of them are going to lose any sleep over sentencing him," Arturo pronounced confidently.

If I were in the jury room looking over the court transcripts, remembering how flat and nearly catatonic Deborah's testimony was, as Ripley went over and over the same questions, getting the same 'details' over and over, and then Rodriguez kept to short questions with his cross, and Deborah did not deny any of the incidences of violence she initiated; I would have reasonable doubt. I imagine it is tough for Gustavo to sit through this, but he needs not to look like Rodriguez has lost already, Ioan reflected.

SAN ANTONIO TUESDAY AFTERNOON

LEONIDAS PULLS HIS CAR UP THE DRIVEWAY LEADING TO Ioan's apartment door. Looking around the outside and checking the door, he found everything secure. He checked the mailbox and pulled out a handful of junk mail items. *I'm glad Ioan let me know so I can check things out, given that Arturo didn't let him know ahead of time they'd be going to Ozuna this week. Ioan will be relieved to know there have been no break-ins this week. It's been five times in the last two years that his place has been burgled.* Leonidas wondered.

Getting back to his car, he noticed Neil walking up the driveway. *What's he doing here?* Leonidas could sense Neil's presence, which was very unusual, especially as Ioan and Cecilia's childhood attachment was not something Neil had ever been entirely comfortable with. Leonidas recalled

Ioan and Cecilia being accused by Neil of making him a cuckold some years back during a "let's all get drunk" party last year. It was a scene that could have been out of an Edward Albee play.

Neil faced Leonidas with a somber but blank stare. He was pale and rather drawn. His shirt was a wrinkled Pierre Cardin white shirt with the top buttons undone. He was unshaven and looked like he had been up all night.

"Neil, are you alright? What's going on?" Leonidas asked, feeling somewhat confused by Neil's unusual appearance. Even when Neil was doing yard work or relaxing, he was dressed like a GQ male model.

"She's dead. Cecilia died last night," Neil said with his blank stare, looking out over Leonidas' shoulder.

"What happened?"

"I found her last night when I came home. She was sitting in the den with her headphones on. She had been watching that Wim Wender's film Ioan gave her."

"What was it: her heart, a stroke?"

"She had pancreatic cancer. She did not want people to

know. She had been taking oxycontin for the increasing pain. She did not want any of the prescribed chemotherapy. She insisted that her acupuncture treatments were working, but the synthetic opioid made her feel so much better as her condition became worse. So, she overdosed," Neil coolly explained, "I don't think she meant to. We had talked about separating last week because she did not want me to suffer this ending, which she had hinted would happen. I told her no matter what, I would be there for her, but I really wasn't, not the way your brother has been."

"Ioan loved Cecilia, but he never wanted her to be anything but happy with you or anyone she wanted to share herself with. We all share your loss, Neil. What can I do?"

"Nothing. Tell Ioan for me. Arrangements with the Neptune Society are being carried out. Only her sister and I will attend the cremation on Friday. It will be just the two of us," Neil said coldly and turned to walk away.

"Goodbye, Neil. Take care," Leonidas sheepishly farewelled. *That's incredible. None of us knew, and yet we all thought we had known her so well for so long. Cecilia feels no pain now. Poor Neil. He didn't even ask where Ioan was. He's still in shock.*

Back in the Crockett County courtroom, Prosecutor Ripley called her next witness: "We call Barbara Baird, your Honor."

Ioan recognized her as the short-haired blonde woman who had been sitting at the prosecution table. As Ripley requested, she identified herself as a licensed professional sexual abuse counselor and UCLA faculty member. *Ripley is countering my "expertise" with this expert witness. That's why she brought up the bipolar diagnosis* Ioan recalled.

"Prolonged sexual victimization changes brain functioning," Baird explained. "At UCLA, we developed the HAVoSA assessment to gauge a person's level of functioning as a result of enduring episodes of sexual abuse."

"The HAVoSA? What is that?" Ripley asked for the benefit of the court.

"It's the Help for Adult Victims of Sexual Abuse. It is a self-report assessment of six domains and 108 items for female subjects and 104 items for male subjects," Baird expertly replied. *She's half smiling. She's proud of her work on developing that artifact of psychosexual expense,* Ioan surmised.

Baird went into explanations about dissociative symptoms resulting from child sexual abuse. She shared data from research done with the HAVoSA in language the jurors could understand: "As adults, victims become more guarded and less open, or completely withdrawn from everyday social interactions," she explained.

Then came Rodriguez's questioning of Baird:

"Thank you for coming today. Have you talked to Deborah Grijalva?"

"No, I haven't," Baird answered.

"Okay. Is the HAVoSA in widespread use, say, by the American Psychiatric or American Psychological Associations?"

"I can tell you that we have published papers in 2018 and we are finishing another study this year," Baird responded.

"Okay. How does the HAVoSa compare with the Adolescent Clinical Sexual Behavior Inventory as far as its reliability, I mean, does it measure consistent results, and what about its validity? Are its results found to be 'true to life?'" Rodriguez asked in an even and curious tone.

"Well, we have not done any meta-analysis – that's when several studies are studied for finding comparative strengths and weaknesses," Baird responded, turning to the jury.

"Okay. But to the best of your knowledge, Deborah Grijalva has not been administered the HAVoSA; is that correct?"

"No, I have no knowledge of any measurement procedures Ms. Grijalva has been given."

"Okay. Thank you, Ms. Baird."

Judge Cardenas then closed the proceedings and reminded everyone that the trial would resume at ten tomorrow morning.

Ioan and Arturo went back to their hotel, packed up, checked out, and headed back down I-10 to San Antonio. All the way back, Arturo praised Ripley for her "solid prosecution," which he admitted he would not have wanted to defend against. Ioan countered that Rodriguez seem to hold the jury's attention more with his soft spoken and to the point questions, especially how he made Baird's expert testimony appear as irrelevant as Deborah's was doubtful.

_________ MONDAY, FIRST WEEK
OF NOVEMBER

Ioan woke up late. The news of Cecilia's passing was depressing. Still, he took consolation in knowing she would no longer be suffering, and he would carry her memory into his dream life – that would be a good thing, feeling she would be more with him as had been his experiences talking with other survivors of significant losses. He then found a text message on his iPhone from Jakob Milstein sent on Monday when the trial had started:

"Ioan, it's Jake. I might have some good news for you. Give me a call when you get back in town."

Ioan punched Dr. Milstein's contact listing on his iPhone expecting to hear his old friend's welcoming voice – but he didn't.

"Hello, this is Judith Nimoy. Can I help you?"

Ioan recognized her name: she was one of Milstein's daughters. "Hello, Judith, I'm Ioan Apostolos…"

"Yes, my father had spoken of you often." "Had spoken" – something has happened. Judith lives in Florida, Ioan realized.

"I am sorry to tell you my father passed away last Tuesday afternoon. My mother's caregiver found him in his home office sitting in his chair. According to her he appeared to just pass peacefully with a calm expression on his face, as if he fell asleep. He told us about you often. How you helped him with their shopping at Costco once a month, and how the two of you would check out new restaurants together. I feel I know you," Judith exclaimed.

"Judith, my condolences for your family's loss. Your father was, in so many ways, a caring and brilliant man. I will miss him all the days left in my life," Ioan spoke with calm solemnity.

"Thank you, Ioan. I had hoped to meet you, but you just caught me as we were about to leave to go back to Orlando. As you know, Father did not attend synagogue, but we had a memorial service this morning at Temple Bethel. Sorry, you weren't there - we kept it limited to family. I am sorry I did not contact you about it," Judith explained, "His body has been sent to the UT Medical School for medical school students to study."

"Yes, even at the end of his living life, his lifeless body puts him back on his favored work: teaching," Ioan stated with a considered mix of respect and regret. "Take care, Judith. Have a safe trip."

"Thank you, Ioan. If you are ever in Orlando, do look us up," Judith signed off.

Ioan put down his iPhone and stared out the window, observing the murder of boat tails and starlings pecking about his neighbor's lawn. *I will miss Jake. He really cared about me as much as I did him. Sleep well, old friend, till we see each other again.* He opened his laptop and found an email from Leonidas:

"What was the verdict?" the message simply read.

Oh, yeah. I need to call Rachel to find out. This is going to be tough if Rodriguez loses. That will make Arturo happy about being right in his prediction.

"Hello, Rachel. It's Ioan Apostolos. How are you?"

"We are so good! Ioan, the verdict was unanimous: Not Guilty!" Rachel said proudly. "Thank you so much for helping us."

"I thought Rodriguez was very effective, especially when the time came for the jury to consider Ripley's case. I am very happy for you, Gustavo, and your beautiful family. Take care."

Ioan closed the call. *That's a big relief I had almost forgotten to remember, or maybe I wanted to remember to forget it, fearing the worst. Lord giveth, and the Lord taketh away. Blessed be..."*

A loud and forceful knock on the door snapped Ioan out of his internalized wondering. Leonidas and Cathy, his significant other, appeared on the porch. Leonidas presented Ioan with a medium-sized U-haul box.

"We found someone who's been calling your name," Leonidas happily proclaimed.

Looking inside, Ioan saw a small tuxedo coat kitten who looked up at him and vocalized "ee-on."

"We found him at the Yard last night as we were coming out of the Olmos Brews across from the box cars. I think he could be Dharma's brother. See that white spot on his forehead," Leonidas pointed out, "we call him Chakra."